Touching the Nooksack

poems by

Shifra Shaman Sky

Finishing Line Press
Georgetown, Kentucky

Touching the Nooksack

for my parents

Copyright © 2021 by Shifra Shaman Sky
ISBN 978-1-64662-634-2 First Edition
All rights reserved under International and Pan-American Copyright Conventions. No part of this book may be reproduced in any manner whatsoever without written permission from the publisher, except in the case of brief quotations embodied in critical articles and reviews.

ACKNOWLEDGMENTS

Many thanks to Elaine Equi for the inspiration provided by her poem, "Like Banners, My T-shirts Hang," published in her collection *The Intangibles* (Coffee House Press, 2019).

"Chinese Herbs Arrive in Allendale SC, Population 5000" was originally published in the Asian-American journal *asiam*, 1998.

The original version of "Beach Glass" was published in *Poetry Bone,* 1998. "Happy Birthday Baby" was originally published in *5.5 BW,* 2006.

Publisher: Leah Huete de Maines
Editor: Christen Kincaid
Cover Art: A.E. Marlowe
Author Photo: C. Danette Wilson
Cover Design: Elizabeth Maines McCleavy

Order online: www.finishinglinepress.com
also available on amazon.com

Author inquiries and mail orders:
Finishing Line Press
PO Box 1626
Georgetown, Kentucky 40324
USA

Table of Contents

Touching the Nooksack 1

How to Explain the Death of One You Love to Someone Who Will Not Be Hurt by It 2

Lent in the Time of COVID 3

A Dream Recurs 4

Socrates Mounts His Defense in the Form of a Villanelle 5

Chinese Herbs Arrive in Allendale SC, Population 5000 6

Happy Birthday Baby 7

Herat 1979/2001 8

A Vulnerable Eye 9

Invitation via Fortune Cookie 10

Jerrold Had a Strange Occurrence 11

Ancestry 12

On Learning, the Morning After the Fact, What Anne Had Decided to Do to Herself 13

Beach Glass 14

Shredding Day Sestina 15

Desire Like the Atom 17

If Lost Call Katy 18

I Narrate My Life to Enlighten the Studio Audience 19

Like Semaphores, Signaling from the Recent Past 20

Insomnia 21

Hawk 22

"Said the river: imagine everything you can imagine, then keep on going."

Mary Oliver

Touching the Nooksack
    for A.E. Marlowe

I could not remember the last time I touched a river—
no, not even once (unless a child's memory suppressed).
That morning at the Nooksack I reached down to deliver

my benison and, instead, received from the giver
that which I felt must be returned because, in my distress,
I could not recall the last time I caressed a river

with my hand my flesh my body, glimpsed within the mirror
I keep covered as a grieving Jew or look in through a mist—
a misty morning at the Nooksack when I thought I might surrender

to the glacier or the falls or to the jagged ridge, the tower,
as my commemoration of a year begun afresh
because I could not remember the last time I touched a river—

no, not even once (either silty, murky, ever clear).
Not one encounter about which I might later reminisce
entering the cirque formed by the Nooksack as a theater

my performance a soliloquy (of course) that I'd deliver
and, to an audience awaiting revelation, I would blow a kiss.
That morning at the Nooksack when I thought I could surrender
and remembered never in my life did I bend toward a river.

**How to Explain the Death of
One You Love to Someone
Who Will Not Be Hurt by It**

I've discovered it to be a new variety of grief—
this expected recitation of my pain.
No matter who demands it—the spectrum of belief
has set a schedule for sorrow—but in vain.

Yet even with that wound I should be whole enough—
they think—to forfeit what I treasure most in life.
You'll find the finest membrane between life and death is rough
contrasted with the sharpness of that knife.

I'll tell them of a dream I had!—perhaps that will suffice
to satisfy their craving for my soul.
We met upon a bridge at dawn—you offered your advice
on how to navigate exertions to console.

Lent in the Time of COVID

How shall I embrace thee, O Lent?

With a divided heart,
a doubting mind,
and a soul not yet
stripped of defenses?

I shall embrace thee with
arms unused to embracing,
but I shall embrace thee, O Lent.

I shall embrace thee with hesitant hands,
touch thee with trembling fingers.

I shall lay down with thee
on a bed of nails
      of coals
      of ice
and count the ways I fear thee, O Lent.

Art thou the Lent of my life?
Shall I embrace thee without
prayer, without alms?
Shall I fast from
all other embracing?

I hadn't planned on giving up so much.

But I shall welcome the ashes
of your coming and
smudge them round my eyes,
to make myself lovely for you,
O perpetual Lent.

A Dream Recurs

This is the room I've discovered
in a house where I used to live—
as small and as sweet as a cupboard.

Why has no one spoken a word—
its appointments superlative?
This is the room I've discovered

where a cat on the window purred
and screens parcel light like a sieve—
as small and as neat as a cupboard.

There my memories are interred—
is there someone I need to forgive?
This is the room I've discovered

and night after night I have heard
in the chamber that holds me captive—
as small and discreet as a cupboard

the sound that seeps in like no other—
a mournful, magnificent bird?
This is the room I've discovered
as dark and as cramped as a cupboard.

Socrates Mounts His Defense in the Form of a Villanelle

Please disregard the manner of my speech—
you've heard so many lies—you may be shocked
to learn I feel unqualified to teach

the youth of Athens, so never demand payment, like that leech
from Paros—but forgive me, I do not mean to mock
my betters. So—disregard the manner of my speech.

You know Chaerephon, of course—now quite beyond your reach—
he went to Delphi to determine if he should put any stock
in the wisdom of a man who cannot teach

and the oracle assured him—perhaps because I do not screech
from Clouds—yet there you stand, with your arrows nocked,
taking aim! But never mind—the manner of my speech

is not meant to please you, to weep and wail, beseech
as you've come to expect from a man who's on the block.
I know myself unqualified to teach—

yet I can prophesy your doom, being forced to preach!
Still—should you feel yourselves outfoxed
by one who is unqualified to teach,
please—disregard the manner of my speech.

Chinese Herbs Arrive in Allendale SC, Population 5000

Afternoon tea has changed,
invaded by the inscrutable;
Juniper Berries exchanged
for Dragon Eyes.
And what she christens,
crinkle-eyed, her "witch's brew"
of fruit and twig and root
lives on the flame.

She sets the table just the same
but with China capitalized,
imagining the flowing robes;
the curve of fingernails;
the tiny feet.
The licorice is sweet.
She pronounces the name:
Gan T'sao.
The sugar and the cream
unheeded now.

Her son (the priest) remarks
on this in New York during
Coffee Hour, his demeanor
somewhat dour, attitude amazed.
He tugs a collar approaching
the Mandarin and offers me
a condescending smile.

I tell him that I use them too:
Long Yen Roo.

Happy Birthday Baby

although you've forgotten mine
(it was January, dear)
and didn't send a Valentine
or buy for me a bracelet
as you said you wanted to
(to decorate my ankle
as if I belonged to you).

Happy Birthday Buttercup,
I have no expectations
of the kind that you encouraged
in the course of conversations
in the parlor
in the bedroom
on the street or
in the kitchen
("In our future life together . . ."
was the way that you'd begin them).

So it's Happy Birthday Bunny,
thanks for being my confessor
(and for having the good sense to
not leave money on the dresser).
I do wish you health and happiness,
a gala celebration—and
now here's my present to you:
No regrets, no litigation.

Herat 1979/2001

Forgive me for accusing you, my child.

It was so long ago and you were young—
the camera was a novelty.

You burst out of the shadow beneath Alexander's citadel
with brothers cousins friends—all flocked to John, the Englishman.

There was a time when I would look into your captured eyes
and wonder where they found you when the tanks rolled in.

Did you survive another winter—sheltered safe and fed?
So long after the fact I said a prayer for you.

When we heard about your fighters, holed up in the hills,
no medicine but aspirin—my father cried.

> And who is that? Who drew your gaze directly to the lens?
> You were the only boy who dared to look at her—
> bareheaded and almond eyed; her mere presence a dare.

And now I think I see you—grown.
I see you tall and strong—enraged.
I see the cockpit breached—the towers razed.
I see the blade you hold, the throat you slit.
I hear your God reviled.

Forgive me for accusing you, my child.

A Vulnerable Eye

On her lid, concealed in part
behind the sticky fringe of lash,
the stitches gather.

Tears flow over the embankment
of the lower rim. (A tissue tucked
into her sleeve sees frequent service.)

How does it look, she asks.
Not bad, really, just—open,
no dab of pink to seal the corner shut.
(The pearl excised in pursuit of disease.)

It could be reconstructed, she assures me.
But why? The vulnerable eye—sees.

Invitation via Fortune Cookie

Someone will invite you to a karaoke party
In a part of town you've never been.
And you will hesitate—demur—but allow yourself to be convinced,
Dress up more than usual,
And go.

And then you'll be invited to an outdoor celebration
For a couple whom you've never met.
You'll hesitate—refuse—but allow that you could change your mind,
Dress appropriately down,
And go.

Now let's say I invite you to a private little something
At a residence you've never seen.
Would you hesitate—object—allow curiosity to win,
Dress for maximum effect,
And come?

Jerrold Had a Strange Occurrence

He was resting, again, in the lounger
(awaiting the painters' intrusion)
watching the workman, busy with plaster,
and felt a great hand bear down on his brain.

It reached inside—click!—and his mind switched off
(or so he described it the following day;
this was after they had made "beautiful love,
at last," as the wife wrote down in her diary).

They'd left the workman and taken a walk
(he was firm on his feet and he knew her;
but all else was strange—it seemed as if chalk
had created his world, and then met with erasure).

Of course, I wouldn't know any of this if
years later the journal had not gone astray.
(Though she may have forgotten she'd written it,
tucked in the back, so much else ripped away.)

She insisted, he did well enough with an aspirin
(it was all he wanted, she wrote, or confessed).
But die well, I wonder now—no intervention
from what was prescribed, in the medicine chest?

I remembered seeing her, dressed with intention
for mourning dear Jerrold, an unwelcome guest
rather than a husband, with ailments unmentioned,
who seemed, in the end, to his death, acquiesced.

Ancestry

Hanna—grandmother—my mother's mother
left her *shtetl* in Poland in nineteen and twelve
and came to America—lips pressed together.

She wants to be heard—here and now.
She wants to tell why—in brittle photographs—she frowns,
and why she served the chicken—always—upside down
with that dark gaping cavity turned

toward

Joseph—grandfather—my mother's father.
A somewhat careless carpenter,
he held his knife and fork and her
in rough disfigured hands.

A boy—A girl—A boy—one more.
That meal was her revenge—a Sabbath protest
she could relish and survive.

Hanna—grandmother—wants to be heard—here and now.
For me—she says—be powerful.

**On Learning, the Morning After the Fact,
What Anne Had Decided to Do to Herself**

I couldn't get through—
Couldn't lift you.
Didn't have the leverage,
The magical palanca,
That hold on the future.

A predicted effect of
The chosen enclosure?
All of them saved!
So are they holy relics now,
Sprayed with your blood?

It's the ultimate act of aggression,
Said someone—a woman who knew you
Better than I, who sat with you
Through one such night and
Wondered—what could it
Possibly be?

Is it chemical—cyclical—circuitry?
You told her you'd never go
Through it again, and she
Thought—well good!
It won't happen again.

But that's
Not what
You meant.

Beach Glass
    for Melissa Crandall

Stone chips
flat as lentils or
round like pearls
of barley
rinsed in surf—sing

Bearded loaves of stone
are puckered with
the mouths of barnacles
the sand littered with
shell and claw and
glistening weed

And glass—the jagged rim
the slicing edge
worn smooth
in flow and ebb
is washed ashore

Beneath an arc of tern
she leans against a
tug of undertow
and having passed
consistency
measures, in the light,
transparency
and pockets
the prize

Shredding Day Sestina

The week that held what would have been her ninety second birthday,
    Mother's Papers
were consigned to flame—if only. For there had been no dancing
    Flames.
Instead there was an advertised community event—Shredding Day!
The service was gratis—why not take advantage? Crisscrossing
    merciless Teeth
shimmied on the sidewalk in a truck like a cement mixer, a Lions Cage.
What a festive destruction of history, a metaphorical Murder.

Five years Susannah waited, and some months, to plan the Murder,
to be sure nothing was needed. (By whom? To prove what?)
    Mother's Papers
(tax returns, old letters, medical pronouncements) were carted to the
    Lions Cage
(high school yearbooks with autographed names she'd hoped to
    consign to Flames)
Susannah wheeling them (bank statements and diaries) to the
    shuddering Teeth,
stopping to buy ices at a nearby stand to celebrate—Shredding Day!

Balloons announced a carnival environment on Shredding Day;
a bake sale to benefit the local church—a prelude to Murder.
Susannah spared a glance for brownies, marching toward the Teeth,
still harboring a preference for fire, and Mother's Papers
(sentimental greeting cards, a sketchbook) consigned instead to Flames
but of necessity she acquiesced, a Christian to the Lions Cage.

If mother hadn't lingered on her way into the Lions Cage.
If they'd only had a fireplace—too many ifs! Shredding Day
was second best, and intersecting blades as merciless as Flames
(although one couldn't witness one's accomplishment of Murder).
Susannah remained cheated of experience—Mother's Papers
emptied all at once into the bin that fed them to the hidden Teeth.

Why not make it of lucite, the housing for its merciless Teeth?
Or why not employ plexiglass as siding for the Lions Cage,
granting 'Little Susie' satisfaction at the death of Mother's Papers?
But this subtracted just a modicum of joy from Shredding Day
and from the ultimate delight of committing any Murder,
any act resulting in destruction; Susannah relinquished the Flames,

embracing the available alternative to dancing Flames.
Internally she sang a hymn as a recorded life succumbed to Teeth
instead, exulting in the daughter's metaphor of Murder—
the final sum of someone's life surrendered to the Lions Cage.
Remembering the night, so long before she knew of Shredding Day,
where—notified by staff—she signed what became the last of
    Mother's Papers.

Where she, dreaming of Flames, had not been welcome,
    Mother's Papers
waited in seclusion for the day—Shredding Day!—for chomping Teeth
bared in the Lions Cage, 'Little Susie' licking ice, savoring Murder.

Desire Like the Atom

Desire, like the atom, is explosive with creative force:
A tiny crumb that secrets others on a planetary course.

But crack the shell, the risk is yours to blossom or to burn:
A fatal misconception spikes an inflorescent crown.

Desire's adaptation is a wobbly ellipse:
A nebula that reeled to give it birth our only glimpse.

If Lost Call Katy

A photocopied notice, fixed to
a post with electrical tape and

fringed with Katy's number—the clipped strips
snapping like pennants in a brisk March breeze.

It concerned her finding of a necklace, or was it a one-eyed
cat, neither of which I'd been missing.

All the same I tore off one little lifeline and
tucked it into a pocket, because I had lost—something.

A breast.
My breast.

Not carelessly misplaced but a theft assented to,
my signature upon a dotted line.

If lost call Katy—an invitation if ever I heard one!
And so, an R-S-V-P.

Hello? I said.
I'm lost.

I Narrate My Life to Enlighten the Studio Audience
(It Isn't Easy to Be Fascinating)

We were making sandwiches.
I took care of the tomatoes,
providing commentary as I sliced.

What are you doing?
I am narrating for the benefit of the studio audience.

You must have been satisfied,
remembered I like cooking shows
(you asked no further questions).

But I have always done this—
a serious child, five or six,
altering the flow of water in the
bathroom sink, wriggling fingers
under the faucet, tapping the aerator.

How long have you been doing this?
Jimmie asked, mesmerized.

Oh, a couple of years.
I was nonchalant, as members of the
Mouse's Club gathered around me.

And, when older, walking home from junior high,
I'd click my tongue to indicate the audience
had just tuned in to catch the conversation.
Whichever friend it was found this annoying:
Stop doing that!

I have not stopped (though, with advanced technology, I need only blink).

But you, O Lord, have searched me out and know me.
You are always there and I am grateful (and it makes me cringe).

You must be glad you came, I'll say,
as I place a small round bandage
over the laptop's omnipotent eye.

Like Semaphores, Signaling from the Recent Past
in conversation with Elaine Equi

I never wore them in public—
not after that instance of recognition
on my way to the grocery store.

That year's model, turquoise and white.
A chest-wide logo on its face,
STAFF emblazoned on the back.

"Look," one woman said to the other,
"we know her, she works at _____,"

but I passed without acknowledgment,
hoping they wouldn't realize I'd heard.

After this encounter I continued to covet
them as each summer approached in

Bright Red or Yellow
Navy or Burgundy
Olive or Some Other Green

but in extra-large sizes for sleeping.

The annual flags of my former employment
still waving to me in my dreams.

Insomnia

No Novocain is needed for
this long deep-rooted pain.
A ruly tongue not worrisome;
No pleasure there to gain.

No probe will pierce the darkness of
this endless dreamless night.
An idle hand not in demand;
a bird unpoised for flight.

No notice need be taken at
this moment of rebirth.
An open heart not set apart;
a soul returned to Earth.

Hawk

Into my cramped narrow kitchen I stepped with
purpose to fetch—something—and saw, at its far end

>   (as if through a telescope,
>   trained on the lone window)

a hawk standing sentry on the topmost rail of my fire
escape. And though the gate was closed and the blinds
were down, I could see her clearly through the latticework
of crossing bars and slats.

How could something so wild, so unexpected, be *right there*,
little more than an arm's length from the kettle on the stove?
And when she lifted her wings—oh, she was magnificent.

And gone.

Shifra Shaman Sky worked for several years as a textile designer, creating patterns stitch by stitch on graph paper scaled to 100 boxes per square inch. At first glance these strict parameters might seem to limit a designer's scope, but she enjoyed the challenge and carried the process into her writing, first endeavoring to work within the scaffolding of the Villanelle, Sestina, and other poetic forms to articulate a wide range of experiences and communicate her close observations of daily life.

Also a painter, Shifra studied at New York's School of Visual Arts in the 1980s, and exhibited her work at a Manhattan gallery. She both entered and exited a convent in the 1990s, and was employed most recently as website administrator for a local nonprofit.

Shifra has contributed to publications as varied as *Voices Found: Women in the Church's Song* (Church Publishing 2003) and *Letters to J.D. Salinger* (University of Wisconsin Press 2002). She holds an MFA from New York University where she studied both fiction and poetry.

www.ingramcontent.com/pod-product-compliance
Lightning Source LLC
LaVergne TN
LVHW041522070426
835507LV00012B/1769